Out of
DARKNESS
into
Light
The Price of Redemption

Sherrita X

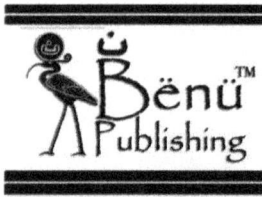

Bënü™ Publishing

Published with love by Benu Publishing

an entity of A Phoenix Rising Wellness Institute.

www.benupublishing.com

ISBN 978-1-926436-09-8

Registered in Canada.

Printed in the United States of America

DEDICATION

In first giving the glory, praise and honor to the Lord of the Worlds, I am thankful to be able to write these words of Dedication to all of the invaluable people who have showed me unconditional love through their duty- especially the Honorable Minister Louis Farrakhan, his loving wife, Mother Khadijah Farrakhan and their family who have sacrificed unselfishly so that we can live.

This is also dedicated to the loving memory of my mother Millie, my brother Kenny, and to my Grandmother Sammie Bell- whose love and life transcends the grave- as they live through me.

This is dedicated to my father, Kenneth Sr., who continues to encourage and inspire me with his encompassing love.

And last, but not least, this is dedicated to my wonderful five children -for they are truly my heroes and they are the answers to all of my prayers...

PREFACE

In the Name of Allah, The Beneficent, The Merciful, I am thankful that I was Blessed to hear a word from the Honorable Minister Louis Farrakhan that has changed my life forever. Also, I am eternally grateful that he has been a wonderful example for all of us. He has paid the Price of Redemption and walked from Darkness into the Light of Freedom, Justice and Equality!

Sherrita X, Author

TABLE OF CONTENTS

FOREWORD

This book was written by Sister Sherrita X. She is a mother and grandmother dedicated to the upliftment of fallen humanity.

She presents information that can inspire us to pay the Price of Redemption that will lead us from Darkness into Light.

Just think of all the blessings and success that are guaranteed for those of us who actively choose and participate in our own self-improvement. This is a Great Day for the Righteous!

Dorothy J. Muhammad

ON THE GIVING OF PRAISE

According to the story as given to us in the Bible in the Book of Matthew, Chapter 21, verses 14 through 16, while Jesus was in Jerusalem visiting the Temple and driving out those who were desecrating it, the blind and the lame came to him and he took time to heal them. As the children watched all of this in wonderment, they began to weep and cried out in praise, *"Hosanna (Halleluia), to the Son of David!"* [a]

The chief priests and scribes, in hearing this and seeing the works of Jesus, said to him, *"Do you hear what they say?"* to which he replied, *"Haven't you ever read the Scriptures? For they say, 'You have taught children and infants to give you praise.'" (Psalms 8:2)*

Are we not the figurative "children" spoken of in this scripture? Are we not the "Children of Israel"? Are we not witness-bearers to a mighty work that is being done today, among the people? Is there not a healing of the "blind" (Spiritually Blind) and the "lame" (Inability to do for Self) today?

Are we not bearing witness and praising the Lord of the Worlds for sending One who would come into the "Temples" (Churches, Mosques, Synagogues) and throw out the imbibers of our wealth, who sell us a lie and the thieves who profit off of our miserable condition?

Within the pages of this book, you will discover that Sis. Sherrita shares her beautiful expression of faith and praise.

Through the sharing of wisdom from the words of the Teachings of The Most Hon Elijah Muhammad through His Greatest student, the Hon Min Louis Farrakhan, one can easily follow her thoughts and delve deeper into the ideas presented within this simple and true little book.

Working with her on getting this project to you, was such an honor. It has been a labor of love and we pray that you enjoy reading this, finding your own true expression of this tremendous wisdom and praising the Lord of the Universe with your own bearing of witness today! Arise, you Children of the Most High God, alas, your Faith without works is Dead!~

Sis Tisa Muhammad, Publisher

To the Mothers of Civilization

*Oe&W*hat amazing women we have been and are destined to become! I thank Allah who appeared to us in the Person of Master Fard Muhammad. We did not have the true knowledge of God before Master Fard Muhammad's coming to raise up a Divine leader, teacher and guide for us. We only had what our former slaves master had given us of ourselves and of God before the coming of our Deliverer, Master Fard Muhammad.

He specially prepared and taught The Honorable Elijah Muhammad for 3 1/2 years the true Knowledge of Allah (God) and the true knowledge of ourselves.

The Book of Matthew 24: 27, 28 reads,
"For as the lightning cometh out of the east, and shineth even unto the west; so shall also the coming of the Son of man be. For where so ever the carcass is, there will the eagles be gathered together."[b]

So what is a *carcass*? It is the dead body of an animal, especially one slaughtered for food. The body of human remains from which the substance or character is gone: the carcass of a once glorious empire. Metaphorically, this could also mean a people who were made dumb, deaf and blind. They have become a nation of people-- like a dead carcass—making no motion.

Yes, the "carcass" that the eagle was flying over in Matthew 24, represents the *mentally and spiritually* dead original nation. Our nation has been made mentally and spiritually dead by a slavery teaching which elevated the Caucasian (white) people and demonized the so- called (Negro) Black people. Therefore, it is not by accident that this nation of people today are being held captive in America, whose symbol is *the bald eagle*.

The Bald Eagle Symbol

ow, let's talk about the bald eagle. The bald eagle was chosen June 20, 1782, as the emblem of the United States of America. One of the many reasons why it was chosen was because of its long life, great strength and majestic look, as well as because it was then believed to exist only on this continent (North America).[1]

The bald eagle does not generally feed on chickens or other domestic livestock, but it will make use of available food that of dead and decaying flesh. According to Wikipedia[2] it is reported that Benjamin Franklin said, in a letter written to his daughter Sarah Bache January 26, 1784, from Paris, criticizing the Society of the Cincinnati, he stated his personal distaste for the bald eagle's behavior.

In the letter Franklin states:

---

[1] Source www.baldeagleinfo.com /eagle/eagle9.html

[2] http://en.wikipedia.org/wiki/Bald_eagle

"I wish the bald eagle had not been chosen for the representative of our country. He is a bird of bad moral character. He does not get his living honestly..."

The bald eagle is an opportunistic carnivore with the capacity to predate a great variety of prey.

According to Webster, *Prey* is defined as, *"an animal hunted or seized for food, especially by a carnivorous animal; A person or thing that is the victim of an enemy, a swindler a disease etc; the action or habit of preying a beast of prey; to seize and devour prey as an animal does (usually followed by on or upon) to exert a harmful or destructive influence; to victimize another or others."*

This predatorial behaviour can be observed in life. For example, *"loan sharks"* prey upon the poor. Now, ponder that! Then I looked up the meaning of the word *carnivorous*. It means *"one who victimizes or injures others; a predator"*.

As I was reading about the *carnivorous animal/person*, I thought about the scripture in the Bible, found in the book of Genesis 15:13ᶜ.

In it, Allah (God) was speaking to Abram, *"And He said unto Abram, Know of a surety that thy seed shall be a stranger in a land that is not theirs, and shall serve them; and they shall afflict them for four hundred years; And also that nation, whom they shall serve, will I judge: and afterward shall they come out with great substance."*

This Scripture is describing a people being held as slave in a strange land for four hundred years (under the oppressive mind of human predators). These people are called, "The Children of Israel".

The Real Children of Israel

The Honorable Minister Louis Farrakhan really helps us to understand the meaning of that prophetic scripture (Genesis 15:13) in his lecture, "Who are the True Children of Israel? Blacks are the True Children of Israel". The Honorable Minister Louis Farrakhan delivered this monumental subject at the Civic Center in Atlanta, Georgia on June 26, 2010.

In that lecture, The Honorable Minister Farrakhan stated that, *"The Most Honorable Elijah Muhammad has said that Almighty God Allah revealed to him that the Black people of America are The Real Children of Israel, and we are The Choice of God; and that unto us He will deliver His Promise.*

This question, says that somebody has usurped our position. This question says that somebody has taken The Promise of God to the Children of Israel, and claimed it for themselves."

The Minister continued, *"But those of you who are scholars of Christianity, Judaism and Islam: If you can disprove this, then I'll pay with my life for lying.*

To all of those who feel that the Children of Israel are over in that place they call "Israel": You are mistaken.

But the wickedly wise have known The Truth; and because they know The Truth, and they know The Time, they are working night and day to trick you out of The Promise of God, and take you down to hell with them, because The Time of Their End has come!

The Architecture of White Supremacy will have to be exposed, so the Tree of White Supremacy can die, and the Tree of Humanity can live."

The Honorable Minister Farrakhan He stated, *"Master W. Fard Muhammad first made Himself Known to a people who were thought to be no people at all, who were slain from the foundation of this world and are the descendants of slave parents who were stolen from their native land and people who was brought across the Atlantic Ocean on a westerly course.*

They were tortured and murdered physically and mentally and confined to bondage, as we are today, by the last manifestation of the Races, bio-genetically produced to take over the rule of our planet conquering all of its Original Inhabitants and other life species for a limited period of time."

Here are some scriptural references that prophesied of our enslavement:

Isaiah 49:25[d] King James Version (KJV): *"But thus saith the LORD, Even the captives of the mighty shall be taken away, and the prey of the terrible shall be delivered: for I will contend with him that contendeth with thee, and I will save thy children."*

Malachi 4:5[e], The Great Day of the LORD it reads, *"Behold, I will send you Elijah the prophet before the coming of the great and dreadful day of the LORD And he shall turn the hearts of the fathers to the children, and the hearts of the children to their fathers, lest I come and smite the earth with a curse."*

Habakkuk 3:3[f] (KJV), *"God came from Teman and the Holy One from Mount Paran. His glory covered the heavens and the earth was full of his praise. And his brightness was as the light, he had horns coming out of his hand and there was the hiding of his power."*

Why did he hide his power? Why did Master Fard Muhammad allow Himself to suffer for us? We are taught that when He allowed Himself to be jailed that He called for The Honorable Elijah Muhammad so that he could see what he would have to go through if he wanted to see his people free.

The Honorable Elijah Muhammad suffered much persecution. He went through being vilified as a liar and hater. Also, he went to jail and was on the run because of the hypocrites. Even some of his own family tried to kill him.

Master Fard Muhammad and the Honorable Elijah Muhammad were examples for our beloved minister, The Honorable Minister Louis Farrakhan. He is still paying the price for us to be free. His character is being assassinated as he works through sickness and health, night and day to see his people free.

Realistically, this is a Man of God who is working for the good of humanity. He is the *Good tree in our midst*, who has been tried and tested like no one else before him.

The Bible gives us a clear direction of how we can tell the "Good tree" from the "Bad tree" in our midst, as stated in the *Book of Matthew 7*, 15-20[g] *"Beware of false prophets, which come to you in sheep's clothing, but inwardly they are ravening wolves. Ye shall know them by their fruits.*

Do men gather grapes of thorns, or figs of thistles? Even so every good tree bringeth forth good fruit; but a corrupt tree bringeth forth evil fruit. A good tree cannot bring forth evil fruit, neither can a corrupt tree bring forth good fruit. Every tree that bringeth not forth good fruit is hewn down, and cast into the fire. Wherefore by their fruits ye shall know them."

In *Self-Improvement Study Guides: Self Improvement is the Basis for Community Development, Study Guide 13: The Price of Redemption,* The Honorable Minister Louis Farrakhan said, *"There is no reform school, there is no prison, there is no penal institution that can reform nothing and this is why to undertake to reform something that has already been made wrong, there has to be a special redemption and a special redeemer."*

What is Redemption?

We must ask ourselves, *"What is redemption?" Redemption* is the *action of saving or being saved from sin, error, or evil.* Other words associated with redemption are *ransom, salvation* and *deliverance.* A *ransom* is *a sum of money or other payment demanded or paid for the release of a prisoner.*

Salvation is *deliverance from sin and its consequences.* Also, it is *deliverance from harm, ruin, or loss.*

The Honorable Minister Louis Farrakhan teaches us in Study Guide 13: *The Price of Redemption:* "to *redeem means to buy back. This suggests that the item being bought back was once owned by the buyer and for some reason he has temporarily lost possession of it. So, a price has to be paid for the object to be returned.*"

So, now we must ask the question. "*What is the price of the redemption of a people who belong to Allah God but have become captive in the hands of strangers; who have gone astray from the path of Allah God and are living a life contrary to Allah God and contrary to the nature of themselves?* Whether we accept it or not, living the contrary life has caused the people to become savages.

We are asked the question in our lessons, "*What is a savage*"? The answer is a person who has lost the knowledge of himself and who is living a beast life. One thing for sure, a savage needs a *Redeemer*.

Specifically, a Redeemer has to be prepared with a special message to resurrect a savage. Preparation means, "*a measure by which one prepares for something. The act of preparing to put in proper condition or readiness. Planning and making ready for something expected or possible*".

Here are some scriptures that are related to Redemption:

- Holy Quran Surah 9 Al Bara'at (The Immunity), ayat 88-89[h]: *"But the Messenger and those who believe with him strive hard with their property and their persons. And these it is for whom are the good things and these it is who are successful...Allah has prepared for them Gardens wherein flow rivers, to abide therein. That is the great achievement."*

- Holy Quran Surah 33, Al Ahzab (The Allies), ayah 29[i]: *"And if you desire Allah and His Messenger and the abode of the Hereafter, then surely Allah has prepared for the doers of good among you a mighty reward"*.

- Holy Quran Surah 33 Al Ahzab (The Allies), verses (ayat) 43, 44[j]: *"He it is who sends blessings on you, and (so do) His angels, that He may bring you forth out of darkness into light. And He is ever Merciful to the believers."*

- Holy Quran Surah 33 Al Ahzab (The Allies), verse (ayah) 44[k]: *"Their salutation on the day they meet Him will be, Peace! And He has prepared for them an honourable reward".*

Now family, the word *"honourable"* means, *"possessing or characterized by high principles: honorable intentions worthy of or entitled to honor or esteem consistent with or bestowing honor".*

There is much to be studied within the origin of the word itself. When looking at the etymological references to the word *honor*, the following is noted: *honor, (n) circa 1200, "glory, renown, fame earned," from Anglo-French honour, Old French honor (Modern French honneur), from Latin honorem (nominative honos, later honor) "honor, dignity, office, reputation," of unknown origin.* [3]

According to the Etymological reference, it is stated that the change of spelling of the word *honour* to *honor* was not recognized until the 17th Century, when the "u" was notably dropped by Noah Webster in his attempts to "reform" the English language as stated here: *"Till 17c., honour and honor were equally frequent; the former now preferred in England, the latter in U.S. by influence of Noah Webster's spelling reforms."*

---

[3] Online Etymology Dictionary, "honor"
(http://www.etymonline.com/index.php?allowed_in_frame=0&search=honor&searchmode=none)

Notably, the word also was used in the late 14th Century to uphold and refer to *"a woman's chastity"*. Therefore the use of this word as a title, by both the Most Honourable Elijah Muhammad and The Honourable Minister Louis Farrakhan, bears further witness to how Allah stylizes his Prophets and Messengers after the attributes found in a woman, especially one who seeks to maintain and uphold her purity, chastity and thus, her *honor.*

When I sounded out the word, *honorable,* you can hear two other words that are within the word-honorable. When it is sounded as *HON-OUR-ABLE*, we can easily identify the sounds of OUR and ABLE.

"OUR" means, *belonging to or associated with the speaker and one or more other people previously mentioned or easily identified. Belonging to or associated with people in general.*

"ABLE" means *having necessary power, skill, resources, or qualifications; qualified: Having unusual or superior intelligence, skill, such as an able leader. Showing talent, skill, or knowledge: an able speech legally empowered, qualified, or authorized now.*

The word *Hon-our-able* contains a message for all who are striving for righteousness. If we *follow the right way,* we will have an *honorable reward* which is to be raised from a mentally dead state.

Earlier, I quoted from the Holy Quran Surah 33 Al Ahzab (The Allies), ayah 29: *"And if you desire Allah and His Messenger and the abode of the Hereafter, then surely Allah has prepared for the doers of good among you a mighty reward".*

I believe that the *mighty reward* and the great achievement is that we will be *resurrected from a dead state* and we will take on the *characteristics of a redeemer*. We become purified and legally empowered, qualified, and authorized by the Lord of the Worlds to become a Redeemer.

"And those who believe in Allah and His messengers, they are the truthful and the faithful ones with their Lord. They have their reward and their light. And those who disbelieve and reject Our messages, they are the inmates of hell."

~Surah 57 Al Hadid (Iron), ayah 19 [1]

Mud as a Means of Purification

ccording to the Holy Qur'an, Surah 26, Al Hijr (The Rock), ayah 26[m], Allah states, *"And surely We created man of sounding clay, of black mud fashioned into shape."* Thus, it would seem logical that this would be the best means, according to Allah, by which one seeking purification can be made *pure.*

Brother Jabril Muhammad writes in his book *Closing The Gap,* page 41[n], *"Brother Minister, several times in the 1960s and the early 1970s, the Honorable Elijah Muhammad, at His table both in Chicago and in Phoenix spoke about mud. Sometimes He would talk about mud as that which the wicked put on him. On other occasions He would talk like Allah (God) was putting the mud on Him.*

He would use the word mud in very interesting ways. He said and wrote that he was to live, for a time, the life that we live and he explained the reasons why this had to be. The implications of his words are that certainly after he met Allah (God), he would live a life seemingly like us, in some respects, but with Wisdom Allah (God) would have by then brought to him and would Later lift him up from this life..."

"Minister Farrakhan: *"When the Honorable Elijah Muhammad met with Master Fard Muhammad, he said he was so deep in the mud that only his eyeballs were out of the Mud. This means to me that he was covered with mud. He talked about his people being in the mud of civilization.*

Well, what is mud? Mud is earth that is full of water, it is not firm. If you stand on it, you will sink. He said the people threw mud at him, and then you said he said sometimes Allah (God) put mud on him.

The thought that came to me was an ayat of the Holy Qur'an, "Betake yourself to the mud." In that state, when you place mud on your skin, allow it to dry and then take it off, it becomes a means of Purification. That means to me, enemies who look for things to muddy your reputation–if they throw enough mud on you and you survive it–it will be a means of your own purification.

So mud-slinging– in the cheap sense– is when people throw things at each other that they know of one another's weakness or fault or sin. That is called mud-slinging.

Why did the Honorable Elijah Muhammad say, "if they took out full page ads and cursed Him out, word for word and line by line, they would only be helping Him?

His whole attitude toward mud was different from one who is like a child playing in mud. The child comes in and gets mud all over the floor and all over the furniture. This enrages the mother because she has to clean it up.

The Honorable Elijah Muhammad's attitude toward Mud was that no matter what they slung at him, it only ended up being a means of his purification, which was also a means of his elevation. Since that was his attitude, what should our attitude be? It should be the same as his".

So when we are going through a trial we should remember that the trials are only to make us better and to bring out the best in us and the only way that we can overcome a trial is to face it and to know that with the help of Allah God we can overcome any trial.

We Can't Rise Higher than the Condition of Our People

I remember growing up in New York as a child. I was saddened by the alcohol, drug addiction and dysfunction, not only in my family, but also in my community. Back then you could walk down the street on any given day and see our brothers and sisters nodding, looking like they were going to fall but somehow by the grace of God they would always get back up.

I would look at them and I would pray to God to help them. I'm telling you I felt their pain. Looking back the only thing I knew was that I felt their pain.

I understood how they felt because I felt the same way inside. I understood their pain. I didn't know at that time that I was *praying for myself*, meaning that *we cannot rise higher than the condition of our people.*

The Honorable Elijah Muhammad taught us that *"a Nation cannot rise any higher than its women"*. He stated that, *"When you teach a man you teach an individual, but when you teach a woman you teach a Nation."* Also, he stated that *"75% of the work is with the woman"*.

When we look at the *condition* of our people and the communities where we live, we can see that it is indeed *time for the women to rise.*

Master Fard Muhammad stated the following, in The Supreme Wisdom Lessons, Instructions given to the Laborers of Islam in #12.° The M.G.T. and G.C.C., *"I can sit on top of the world, and tell anyone that the most beautiful Nation is in the Wilderness of North America; but do not let me catch any sister other than her own self, in regards to living the life and weighing properly."*

We are the mothers of civilization who must again be restored to their exalted place *back on top of civilization.*

We have the duty to help save our children and a fallen humanity. We must save our children now, we must consider that our open enemy has worked day and night to keep this from happening. The woman has been removed from the home. She is no longer able to teach and rear her children in the way that they should be taught.

Truth is we has given our children over to the hands of our open enemy who is now setting many traps for our children. Just as every creature in creation has an enemy, so do the original people. we can no longer lie to our children about who their enemy is.

The Honorable Elijah Muhammad has taught us that if a man does not treat you right, he will not teach you right. Certainly, we can point to many accounts of mistreatment and injustice done to our people. The fact of the matter is that we must stop pointing and blaming others for our condition.

We must not depend on others for what we can do for ourselves. Yes, family it's just time for us to do something for ourselves --no more marching, no more begging for jobs because it's time to build a nation and do for self.

The Book of Proverbs 22:6ᴾ, *"Train up a child in the way he should go: and when he is old, he will not depart from it."*

So, the question is, *"have we trained our children in a righteous way of life or have we just handed them over to our open enemy"*? If the answer is *yes*, what price are we willing to pay to get them back?

"And when We made a covenant with the Children of Israel: You shall serve none but Allah. And do good to (your) parents, and to the near of kin and to orphans and the needy, and speak good (words) to (all) men, and keep up prayer and pay the poor-rate. Then you turned back except a few of you, and you are averse."

~Surah 2, Al Baqarah (The Cow), ayah 83[q]

The Lioness & Her Cubs

Ezekiel 19, verse 1^r says, *"Take up a lament concerning the princes of Israel and say: 'What a lioness was your mother among the cubs. She brought up one of her cubs, and he became a strong lion. He learned to tear the prey and he devoured men. The nations heard about him, and he was trapped in their pit. They led him with hooks to the land of Egypt."*

The story of this lioness and her cubs continues...

Ezekiel 19: 5^s *"'When she saw her hope unfulfilled, her expectation gone, she took another of her cubs and made him a strong lion. He prowled among the lions, for he was now a strong lion. He learned to tear the prey and he devoured men. He broke down their strongholds and devastated their towns. The land and all who were in it were terrified by his roaring.*

Then the nations came against him, those from regions round about. They spread their net for him, and he was trapped in their pit. With hooks they pulled him into a cage and brought him to the king of Babylon.

They put him in prison, so his roar was heard no longer on the mountains of Israel. "Your mother was like a vine in your vineyard planted by the water; it was fruitful and full of branches because of abundant water.

Its branches were strong, fit for a ruler's scepter. It towered high above the thick foliage, conspicuous for its height and for its many branches. But it was uprooted in fury and thrown to the ground. The east wind made it shrivel, it was stripped of its fruit; its strong branches withered and fire consumed them.

Now it is planted in the desert, in a dry and thirsty land. Fire spread from one of its main branches and consumed its fruit. No strong branch is left on it fit for a ruler's sceptre."

I really love the way this chapter opens up. It starts out by talking about taking up a *lament* concerning the Princes of Israel.

A *prince* is a general term for *a ruler, monarch, or member of a monarchy*. Lament means *a passionate expression of grief or sorrow and to mourn (a person's loss or death)*.

This scripture further expounds upon the strong lioness and how she reared one of her cubs to become a powerful lion. He became so strong that the nations heard of him and laid a trap in a pit and led him with hooks to the land of Egypt.

I was recently asked to speak at the *"Women Who Stood For Freedom"* Conference in Washington, D.C., where I was asked to present something on Harriet Tubman.

As I began to study the life of our dear sister Harriet Tubman, I realized that the system has not changed very much since the time of our enslavement here in the *hells of North America*, especially when it came to the black women and her male child.

Back then, the black woman was always concerned about her male children, knowing that anytime a slave would stand up to the injustices, that he would be killed and made into an example for the other slaves, so in that way the system has always used fear tactics as a means of keeping the slaves in line.

The same tactics are being used today anytime a black person, or rather, any person who stands up for justice concerning the blackman, as they will assuredly be crucified by the media and, or straight out killed.

So the black woman has always protected her male child, which in most cases, made him more dependant on her, weakening him and his nature to rule, and the female child, was left to fend for herself, having to be strong, continuing the cycle with her own male children.

Today, we can see this still remains in our community, so it is now apparent that the black man and woman must be completely made over again so that we can produce a Nation of Gods as opposed to "dogs" and the made-man's "niggers".

The Cubs of the Lioness

I must confess that as I was reading the scripture about the Lioness and Her Cubs, I could not help but see the similarities of these scriptures and the condition of we, the Black people here in the *hells of North America.*

So in my own words of course, the mother was sad when she saw that her hope was un-fulfilled, she took another one of her cubs and made him a strong lion.

He prowled among the lion; he learned to tear his prey and became a man-eater and he broke down their strongholds and devastated their towns; the land and all who were in it were terrified by his roaring.

Then the nations came against him, those from regions roundabout they spread their net for him, and he was trapped in their pit.

Then they pulled him with hooks into a cage and brought him to the king of Babylon. I was thinking in my mind that they put him in prison, and we can see that happening in our own communities every day.

It's so common now that it has become like a badge of honor. Courts are giving our sons life sentences like never before and just like the lion in this scripture their roars are never heard again. It goes on to talk about the mother and how she was a vine - in your vine -yard planter that was fruitful and full of branches of abundant water. Its branches were strong, fit for a ruler's scepter.

It towered high above the thick foliage, conspicuous for its height and for its many branches. But it was uprooted in fury and thrown to the ground. The east wind made it shrivel; it was stripped of its fruit; its strong branches withered and fire consumed them.

Now it is planted in the desert, in a dry and thirsty land. Fire spread from one of its main branches and consumed its fruit. No strong branch is left or fit for a ruler's scepter.

Again I'm looking at *all the traps that are being laid for our sons and daughters today*, black on black crime, the killings of our sons and daughters, police brutality, self-hatred, poor education, the mothers and fathers who are mourning the senseless killings of their children as well as our own dis-unity.

When I speak of dis-unity, I mean we as a people can't seem or won't come together to pool our resources and solve our own problems. It seems to me that we have sympathy for everyone else but ourselves.

We know and sympathize for the so called Jewish holocaust, while most of us know nothing about our own history, especially, the Black Holocaust. It is because we haven't been taught about it and we can't teach our children so that they can say never again. just like the so called Jews.

We send our children to school to learn nothing except how to graduate and get a "good job". When they don't have a degree or become dropouts, they are considered to be nothing in the eyes of our open enemy. Even worse, they too, have taken on that same mindset. Specifically I'm talking about the mind of a white supremacist mindset.

"How doth the city sit solitary, that was full of people! how is she become as a widow! She that was great among the nations, and princess among the provinces, how is she become tributary!

She weepeth sore in the night, and her tears are on her cheeks: among all her lovers she hath none to comfort her: all her friends have dealt treacherously with her, they are become her enemies. Judah is gone into captivity because of affliction, and because of great servitude: she dwelleth among the heathen, she findeth no rest: all her persecutors overtook her between the straits.

The ways of Zion do mourn, because none come to the solemn feasts: all her gates are desolate: her priests sigh, her virgins are afflicted, and she is in bitterness. Her adversaries are the chief, her enemies prosper; for the LORD hath afflicted her for the multitude of her transgressions: her children are gone into captivity before the enemy."

~ Bible, Book of Lamentations 1: 1-5[t]

Delivering Our Children from the Snares of Tricks & Lies

ow, one of the things I have noticed about the story of the Lioness and Her Cubs is that the first lion they laid a trap in their pit for him and led him with HOOKS to the land of Egypt. So I started to look at the word hook and really what is a hook?

It is defined as a piece of metal or other material, curved or bent back at an angle, for catching hold of or hanging things on. It can also be a thing that is designed to catch people's attention.

Like words in a song, consider the music that we allow our children to listen to today. Could the music be a trick to keep our people spiritually and mentally dead? Let us consider the "hooks" in the songs our children are listening to.

They "hook" our children, reel them in and before you know it they're singing along and being programmed to savage thinking. Just think, they tricked some of our people into slavery with the promise of gold and trinkets. What was the end result?

We ended up in a pit. What is a pit? It is an area reserved or enclosed for a specific activity, in particular area. As a mother, and grandmother I see the pit that has been created for us and our children. I can't just sit back and act like none of this is really happening.

So my plea to the Mothers of civilization is that *we must get up!* We must go to work do something to save our children and secure a future and a place in the sun for our future generations.

Lets us remember that in this scripture, the mother was like a vine in vineyard planted by the water. It was fruitful and full of branches because of abundant water and its branches were strong, fit for a ruler's scepter. It towered high above the thick foliage, conspicuous for its height and for its many branches. It is the water that sustains life.

However, the vine was uprooted in fury and thrown to the ground. The east wind made it shrivel and it was stripped of its fruit; its strong branches withered and fire consumed them. Then it was planted in the desert, in a dry and thirsty land.

Fire spread from one of its main branches and consumed its fruit. No strong branch is left on it fit for a ruler's scepter.'

So what lesson can we learn from this scripture? Now, the mothers of civilization must become that water that sustains life so that we can be just like that lioness.

We must rear up our princes and princesses. We must make them strong so that they can take their rightful place and become fit to be rulers once again. "When you feel that you are in a desolate place." Go where there is water."

Esoterically, water represents *knowledge*. So we must return to where there is water. This means that we must become seekers of knowledge and remember those who have gathered water will never go thirsty!!!"

I remember the Honorable Minister Farrakhan being interviewed on *The Phil Donahue Show*. A woman asked him what we can do to instill in our children and make them better.

What can we do to help? I'm paraphrasing what the women said because my focus is really on the answer that the Honorable Minister Farrakhan gave to the women which was the following words, "If we wish to make our children better- one of the things we have to do is to teach them the knowledge of themselves.

As a little boy he said, *"My blessed mother kept instilling in me the love and the pride of being black. She made me to know my history, to know my roots. So I grew up with a love for myself and secure within myself, never feeling inferior and certainly not feeling superior.*

But that chip on the shoulder that the young lady spoke about is my self-assurance, my confidence, my ability to speak the truth without fear. I don't bend when I don't have to, I don't scratch where I don't itch, I look white people in the eye and speak honestly and truthfully and candidly and un-hypocritically to you; that's not a chip that's just self-assurance that comes from self- knowledge.

Teach your children that and whether we are here or there, we will be able to make a future for ourselves."

I am thankful that the Honorable Minister Louis Farrakhan has taught us that the woman is the foundation upon which civilization is built.

We do not judge the degree of civilization of the people by a man.

The wise always look at your woman. By looking at your woman, they can tell how highly civilized you are or how uncivilized you are because she is the reflection of your degree of civilization.

"The wise woman builds her house, But the foolish tears it down with her own hands."

~ *Bible, Book of Proverbs 14, verse 1*[u]

Who Needs to be Redeemed From The Prison Houses?

Redeem means to '*buy back*'. This suggests that the item being bought back was once owned by the buyer and for some reason he had temporarily lost possession of it. Thus, a price has to be paid for the object to be returned.

In the Book of Exodus, Chapter 6, it states in both verses 6 & 7ᵛ the following about *The Children of Israel* and Allah God's plan for Redemption:

"*Wherefore say unto the children of Israel, I am the* LORD, *and I will bring you out from under the burdens of the Egyptians, and I will rid you out of their bondage, **and I will redeem you with a stretched out arm, and with great judgments:** And I will take you to me for a people, and I will be to you a God: and ye shall know that I am the* LORD *your God, which bringeth you out from under the burdens of the Egyptians.*"

As stated earlier from *Study Guide 13* , *"What is the price of the redemption of a people who belong to Allah (God) but have become captive in the hands of strangers; who have gone astray from the path of Allah (God) and are living a life contrary to Allah (God) and contrary to the nature of themselves?"*

"And I will bring you in unto the land, concerning the which I did swear to give it to Abraham, to Isaac, and to Jacob; and I will give it you for an heritage: I am the LORD. *And Moses spake so unto the children of Israel: but they hearkened not unto Moses for anguish of spirit, and for cruel bondage."*

~Exodus 6:9,10[w]

Who needs to be redeemed from the prison houses? It is us; *it is our children.* As mothers each of us have something that we must do to save our children and future generations. I was reading a report written by Saki Knafo, a writer for The Huffington Post, an internet-based periodical[4].

His report warns that one in every three black males born today can expect to go to prison at some point in their life, compared with one in every six Latino males, and one in every seventeen white males, if current incarceration trends continue.

These are among the many pieces of evidence cited by the Sentencing Project, a Washington, D.C.-based group that advocates for prison reform. It has compiled a report on the staggering racial disparities that permeate the American criminal justice system.

---

[4] www.huffingtonpost.com

The report was submitted to the U.N. Human Rights Committee in advance of the U.N.'s review of American compliance with the International Covenant on Civil and Political Rights. It argues that racial disparity pervades *"every stage of the United States criminal justice system, from arrest to trial to sentencing."*

Racial minorities are more likely than white Americans to be arrested". The report explains, *"Once arrested, they are more likely to be convicted; and once convicted, they are more likely to face stiff sentences."*

The report's findings lead its authors to conclude that the U.S. is violating the International Covenant on Civil and Political Rights, which states that all citizens must be treated equally under the law.

The U.S. ratified the treaty in 1992. Now, we really don't need any reports to tell us about the inequalities in the American criminal justice system. We see it going on in our communities every day.

We have witnessed the soaring rates of incarceration rate of our black sons and daughters. Black people suffer dramatically in this current criminal justice system. Black men between age 20 and 34 with no high school diploma, for example, are more likely to end up in jail than to have a job, according to a *2010 Pew Charitable Trust study*.

Other statistics show that blacks receive sentences that are 20 percent longer than whites. Studies have long shown that the death penalty is imposed in a discriminatory manner. Police stops and arrests of questionable constitutionality are imposed disproportionately on Black children according to the Bureau of Justice Statistics (BJS).

Incarceration rates are highest for those in their 20s and early 30s. Prisoners also tend to be less educated: The average state prisoner has a 10th grade education, and about 70 percent have not completed high school according to CBS Local Media[5] in Washington DC.

In addition, more alarmingly, according to the National Adult Literacy Survey (NALS) 70% of American inmates read below a 4th grade level.

"And it came to pass on the day when the LORD spake unto Moses in the land of Egypt, That the LORD spake unto Moses, saying, I am the LORD: speak thou unto Pharaoh king of Egypt all that I say unto thee."
~ Exodus 6: 28, 29[x]

---

[5] *washington.cbslocal.com*

Taking Responsibility to Educate Our Children

*A*side from high rates of incarceration, there are fifteen schools that will be closing their doors in D.C. alone at the end of the 2012-2013 as part of a D.C. Public Schools consolidation and reorganization plan.

School officials say they expect to save $8.5 million per year with the "Better for All Schools" plan. The final determination of schools shutting their doors for good comes after more than two months of sometimes heated meetings between school officials and parents of students upset with the proposal. Now, we must be ever alert to the hook of the school closings.

Could the school closings be part of a sinister plan to fill the prisons with more Black children? Let us carefully examine their language.

The school officials are saying "We've spent the last two months combing over every single comment, data point and proposal. "Now it's time for us to look to the future, for us to plan for the best ways that we can support our students."

In addition to multiple meetings with the City and Education Councils, school officials also met with State Board of Education members, union leaders, parent groups, and the U.S. Department of Education staff. *"Although school consolidations are wrenching, The Chancellor announced that he is confident that the decisions will 'ultimately help strengthen D.C. Public Schools, speed education reform and — most importantly — guarantee our children are getting the resources they need for the world-class education they deserve...'"*

Let us ask the question, *"Is it really about education or is it about warehousing our children in prisons for free labor?"* The incarceration rates of our sons and daughters are increasing at an alarming rate. We must begin to look at what is really going on.

Not only do we have to look at it; we must now prepare ourselves to do something about it. The United States has a long history of forcing its prison population to work as part of their punishment, although by no means is it the only country to do so.

The 13th Amendment passed in 1865, abolished slavery and involuntary servitude for everyone except prisoners. Now prisons are privately owned. In 1871, Virginia declared prisoners *"slaves of the state."* The Supreme Court ruled in 1977 that prisoners couldn't form unions or make work demands.

This all led up to the 1980s and 90s where under both a republican president and a democrat, the prison population skyrocketed. Locking up people for lengthy minimum sentences is truly one of the last remaining bipartisan agreements.

Corporations are realizing that they don't need to send jobs overseas to turn a profit any more. No, they didn't have a change of heart and a newfound willingness to share their hard earned profits with their workers.

Instead, they've found a class of people that they can basically use for free. Even better, these people have almost no rights, no protections and no voices. They are numerous and growing every year. Corporations have realized that they are sitting on the largest population of prisoners in the world. My personal conclusion is that it's just modern day slavery.

The Honorable Elijah Muhammad has taught us that the Black man and women had to be completely made over again and the question that comes to my mind is why he said those words? We have to be the change that we want to see in the world and teach our young girls that they are more than their physical derriere (booty). The parents have a duty to work to be perfect examples for our children.

What I'm saying is that we have to get rid of this slave mentality and create something for ourselves. It is time that we come together and unite our resources. Maybe, the school closings, which are considered a setback, can really be an opportunity for our advancement.

Why do I say that? Let us consider we have a nation of many educated professionals. I think we have everything we need. If schools are closing, then we must take responsibility and teach our own children.

We have teachers, doctors and lawyers, The Honorable Minister Louis Farrakhan has stated in his 58 week lecture series, *The Time and What Must Be Done,* that We (Blacks) are the *only* people in America who are trying to force ourselves on other people.

"We have been crying out for jobs! We need jobs! We must have jobs!" We are suffering today because we rejected The Honorable Elijah Muhammad. If we are ignorant in a time like this, then our ignorance will lead to our destruction. We are going to have to get up from where we are and go to work in order for us to survive and prepare a future for ourselves.

The Most Hon Elijah Muhammad: said, *"As a people, we must become producers and not remain consumers and employees."*

Without land there is no production so we have to have land. We have to have the intelligence to extract raw materials out of the land to make products.

He said that God is going to give us the opportunity to replace the White man because he has ruined his right to stewardship When God raises you and gives you power and authority over what you did not create, He is trying you.

Before God punishes out of His abundance of mercy, He always raises among the people a prophet or messenger.

The Honorable Minister Louis Farrakhan stated in his message, *"The Time, "We are at war with forces"* inside ourselves and outside of ourselves. As a people we have to survive.

He said that there's a difference between separation and segregation. Segregation exists when one power is superior to another and forces its policies on the lesser power.

The Honorable Elijah Muhammad's called for Separation and Equality with the best in civilized society. In fact, Separation is voluntarily done on the basis of two equals. This means no slave, thus no master.

Out of Darkness Into Light:

The Price of Redemption

The Price of Redemption: Study Guide #13, was given to the students and followers of the Most Honorable Elijah Muhammad in October 1988, as preparation for the re-dedication of the headquarters of the Nation of Islam, the National Center, also, known as Mosque Maryam, named after the mother of Jesus by the Honorable Minister Louis Farrakhan.

What is the Price of Redemption? I think we can get a look at the purpose, prophets and messengers. Prophets come in the absence of God to guide the people back to the right path, who has gone astray. Messengers have a greater job than prophets in that they come in the presence of God.

They have the job of resurrecting and regenerating nations with the help of God. Jesus was a prophet that showed the example of how one can attain self-mastery.

"And he said unto them, What things? And they said unto him, Concerning Jesus of Nazareth, which was a prophet mighty in deed and word before God and all the people..."

~ Bible, Book of Luke 24:19[y]

So we are in a time, where there is no longer a need for prophets because now we are in the time of the "Presence of God".

Our Saviour and Deliverer came to us in the Person of Master Fard Muhammad and raised up the Honorable Elijah Muhammad to guide us back to the right path. *"God came from Teman, and the Holy One from mount Paran. Selah. His glory covered the heavens, and the earth was full of his praise."*

~Bible, Book of Habakkuk 3:3

They have been so Merciful to us to leave the Honorable Minister Louis Farrakhan in our midst as a wonderful example for us. He has faced many dangers, hardships, and persecution.

Yet, he has remained steadfast and patient despite overwhelming opposition. When we adopt his way and attitude, we can be guaranteed success and victory over our enemies.

According to the *Bible, Book of Isaiah 53: 3- 5^z*:
"He is despised and rejected of men; a man of sorrows, and acquainted with grief: and we hid as it were our faces from him; he was despised, and we esteemed him not. Surely he hath borne our griefs, and carried our sorrows: yet we did esteem him stricken, smitten of God, and afflicted. But he was wounded for our transgressions, he was bruised for our iniquities: the chastisement of our peace was upon him; and with his stripes we are healed."

I am really thankful for the Honorable Minister Louis Farrakhan words in *Study Guide 13* that really provides a road map for us to pay the price of redemption and walk from darkness into light.

These are his words, *"My desire is that all Believers put ourselves in position to be forgiven for all of our sins, that Allah may heal the wounds of the Nation, so that when the house is dedicated, we also stand before the world this magnificent spiritual house, restored, consecrated and dedicated for the rest of our lives in fulfillment of these words in our daily prayers, 'My prayer, my sacrifice, my life and my death are all for Allah, the Lord of the worlds.'*

Family here is where we really have to get some understanding and know exactly what it is that we are saying in this prayer, this is a very powerful prayer and it must not be taken lightly."

So when we make our supplication to Allah (God) we are saying that we are going to give our ALL to Allah all means: The whole of one's fortune, resources, or energy; everything one has.

There are five (5) major steps that MUST be taken immediately by us the Believers, in order to put ourselves in the desired position:

(1) Prayer

An act of communicating with God, such as in devotion, confession, praise, or thanksgiving. And also the Constance remembrance of Allah (God) will keep us on the straight path.

(2) Fasting

Abstaining from food and drink and all sensuous pleasures refraining from indulging in all appetites we are taught that if we can abstain from the things that are natural for us to do such as eating, drinking being with our husbands or wife's at certain times then fasting will help us to disciplined ourselves from what is not pleasing to Allah (God).

(3) The Dietary Law of One Meal a Day

In the Bible it says that He Allah (God) will give us more life abundantly and that He would teach us what foods to eat and what foods to store in our houses.

The Most Honourable Elijah Muhammad said that food we'll keep you here and food can take you out of hear as well and scene we have been taught how to eat the wrong foods, Mentally Physically and Spiritually, by our former slaver masters it is extremely important that we have a dietary law that will give us life more abundantly there is a very high death rate in our communities mostly do to eating the wrong foods.

Family this scripture Jehovah taught Israel how to live, but Israel rebelled against the law of Jehovah handed down to them through Moses, the servant of Jehovah. Please see *How to Eat to Live, Books 1 & 2* by the Most Honourable Elijah Muhammad.

(4) Charity and Sacrifice

"You cannot attain to righteousness unless you spend (in charity) out of what you love." (The Holy Quran 3:92)[aa]

And also the Holy Quran teaches us that we should *"spend out of what God has given us"*, this means that we should use our energy, talent, resources, money, possessions, or whatever we have, to help and to do good to others in the cause Allah (God) Charity is an demonstration of love and benevolence to Allah (God) charity allows us to putt into practice everything that we have learned and it also allows us to give back or to share the love and the mercy that was shown to us this is how we say thank you to All Mighty God Allah.

"Sacrifice" means *"to perform a sacred rite; give up, let go, surrender."*

Sacrifice builds both the character and the will. It humbles us and increases our spiritual development.

(5) Work

So prayer fasting the dietary law charity are all necessary and to some degree a from of sacrifice.

The Honourable Minister said, *"I have prepared Study Guide 13 for you during this Saviours' Day to help us in our efforts to apply these principles of action... So that even as the Mosque is being made ready, we are being made ready for our dedication. Let us work as best we can to purify ourselves, not despairing, becoming disheartened or losing faith".*

Although those powerful words were written by the Honorable Minister Louis Farrakhan in 1988, they are even more important today. We have entered a period of intense darkness. Also we cannot even begin to talk about raising a fallen humanity until we have become resurrected beings. We can accomplish it by our complete Submission to Almighty Allah (God).

The Honorable Minister Louis Farrakhan in *Study Guide 13* further encouraged us to make our word bond by our actions. He wrote, *"I appeal to you in the Name of Allah, to reflect these words, take them into your heart and act upon them. May Allah Bless, Guide and Protect you. May He strengthen you and make you successful in your endeavours to come"*.

Just think- we are years into the future from his words and now we must strive mightily to build schools, hospitals, housing and businesses. This is because the Honorable Elijah Muhammad is a man of tremendous vision.

He knew the schools and hospitals would close down, he knew that the houses would deteriorate so we would need *"something of our own"*.

Yes, the Honorable Elijah Muhammad knew that we needed schools to mould and shape the minds of our children righteously.

We needed hospitals to truly heal our people and we needed decent housing to improve our quality of life on a daily basis. Like the Honorable Elijah Muhammad and the Honorable Minister Louis Farrakhan, we should remain steadfast, faithful and truthful in the midst of overwhelming opposition.

Also, we must remember that although we can acquire farms, factories, banks, money, and good homes, our ultimate aim is to grow to uprightness. This is because the #1 business of the Nation of Islam is the building and re-building of human lives through a physical, mental and spiritual resurrection.

ABOUT THE AUTHOR

A native of Brooklyn, New York, Sheritta X, lovingly called "Sista Shyne" by her peers, is a tremendous daughter of two beautiful parents- Mildred Gamble & Kenneth Vann. Her artistic mother, a writer herself, a singer and an amazing storyteller, nurtured and cultivated her love of writing and music into the very quintessence of her spirit.

Her father was and still serves as her personal life coach, encouraging her to reach the sky of her dreams and achieve larger than life goals, commanding her to focusing on the God within her so that she could be all that she was created to be!~

Sister Sheritta is a Mother of five children, two boys and three girls, all of whom she has been made proud to share in her own personal life stories, she describes them, lovingly, in her own words, "my children (they) were made perfect for me, because, in any trial that I have gone through, they were made to be very loving, very kind, very supportive- they are achievers!"

The granddaughter of a very strong, steadfast Grandmother, Sammie Bell, who gave her an example of how to overcome all obstacles, she too has made herself an exemplary Grandmother to her own three grandchildren, a dynamic part of her life.

Writing is her love! When you read her words in this book, you will discover the pure love she has for Master Fard Muhammad, the Teachings of the Most Hon Elijah Muhammad and the Hon Minister Louis Farrakhan. Sis Sheritta captivates your heart with the simplicity of her questions and the magnificence of her mind, sharing her thoughts and the essence of her soul through the pages of her book.

Currently, Sis Sheritta owns a production company, *Another Clean Glass Production* and co-owns *Wombniversal Studios*, a dynamic graphics, advertising, web building productions suite and can be found filming documentaries, commercials, music videos or expressions of nature on any given day.

I surmise, when you read the passions of her mind, you too will say, "To know her, is to love her…" *Stay tuned…*

~Sis Tisa Muhammad

SCRIPTURAL REFERENCES

---

[a] Matthew 21: 12-16

[b] Matthew 24: 27,28

[c] Genesis 15:13

[d] Isaiah 49:25

[e] Malachi 4:5

[f] Habakkuk 3:3

[g] Matthew 7, 15-20

[h] Surah 9 Al Bara'at (The Immunity), ayat 88-89

[i] Surah 33, Al Ahzab (The Allies), ayah 29

[j] Surah 33 Al Ahzab (The Allies), ayat 43, 44

[k] Surah 33 Al Ahzab (The Allies), ayah 44

[l] Surah 57 Al Hadid (Iron), ayah 19

[m] Surah 26, Al Hijr (The Rock), ayah 26

[n] Closing The Gap, page 41

[o] *The Supreme Wisdom Lessons, Instructions given to the Laborers of Islam* 12.

[p] Proverbs 22:6

[q] Surah 2, Al Baqarah (The Cow), ayah 83

[r] Ezekiel 19, verse 1

[s] Ezekiel 19: 5

[t] Lamentations 1: 1-5

[u] Proverbs 14:1

[v] Exodus 6: 6, 7

[w] Exodus 6:9,10

[x] Exodus 6: 28, 29

[y] Luke 24:19

[z] Isaiah 53: 3- 5

[aa] Surah 3, Al Imran (The Family of Amran) ayah 92